Zero-Trust Security & AI Threat Monitoring

Continuous AI-Driven Protection for Modern Networks

By Joe Correa

Published by Live Stronger Faster

This book is for educational and informational purposes only. The author and publisher are not engaged in rendering legal, financial, tax, or other professional advice. Readers should consult a qualified professional before making any financial decisions.

First Edition

Table of Contents

Table of Contents

Introduction

In the modern digital world, trust has become the most dangerous vulnerability of all. For decades, cybersecurity was built on a simple assumption: once a user or device was inside a network, it could be trusted. Firewalls were placed at the perimeter, passwords granted access, and internal systems operated as if they were safe simply because they were "inside." That model no longer works. Today's networks are sprawling, cloud-based, remote-access environments filled with thousands of connected endpoints, software integrations, third-party services, mobile devices, and artificial intelligence agents that communicate and make decisions on their own. Hackers do not need to break through a front door anymore. They slip in through forgotten credentials, compromised devices, malicious browser extensions, AI-generated phishing attacks, or hijacked cloud sessions. Once inside, they move freely unless the system is designed to assume that nothing is ever trusted. Zero-trust security is the architecture of this new reality, and artificial intelligence is the only technology powerful enough to enforce it at the speed and scale required for modern digital life.

Zero-trust security is not a product or a single piece of software. It is a philosophy, an architecture, and a continuous enforcement system that treats every user, device, application, and data request as potentially hostile. Instead of trusting anyone by default, zero-trust demands constant verification of identity, behavior, and intent. Every click, login, file access, and network request must be validated in real time. This is where AI becomes essential. Humans and traditional security tools cannot analyze millions of signals per second across complex cloud environments, remote workforces, IoT devices, and AI-powered applications. Only machine learning systems can monitor this level of activity, detect subtle anomalies, and respond instantly before damage occurs. In this book, you will learn how zero-trust security and AI threat monitoring work together to create a living, breathing security system that never sleeps, never assumes safety, and never stops learning.

The rise of artificial intelligence has not just empowered defenders; it has supercharged attackers as well. Modern cybercriminals use AI to generate phishing emails, probe networks for weaknesses, automate brute-force attacks, evade detection systems, and adapt in real time to security responses. Malware is no longer static. It changes its behavior based on the environment it finds itself in. Ransomware can now decide which files are most valuable and which backups to destroy. Botnets can coordinate attacks using machine learning models. This means that traditional signature-based security tools, which look for known threats, are increasingly blind to the most dangerous attacks. Zero-trust and AI-driven monitoring flip the advantage back to the defender by focusing not on what something is, but on what it does. Behavior, context, and risk become the foundation of security instead of simple credentials and perimeter defenses.

At the heart of zero-trust security is the idea that access must be earned continuously, not granted once. A user who logs in successfully is not automatically safe for the rest of their session. An AI system monitors how that user behaves, what resources they access, how fast they move, what files they open, and whether their actions match their historical patterns. If something changes, such as a sudden download of thousands of files, a login from a new country, or an unusual command sent to a server, AI models immediately assign risk and can block, isolate, or challenge the user before a breach occurs. This same approach applies to machines, APIs, cloud workloads, and even other AI systems. Every entity on the network becomes a constantly evaluated participant in a security ecosystem governed by intelligent oversight.

Modern networks no longer live inside one building or one data center. They exist across cloud providers, SaaS platforms, mobile devices, home offices, third-party integrations, and AI-powered tools that communicate across the internet. This creates a security nightmare for traditional models that rely on defined boundaries. Zero-trust replaces boundaries with identity, context, and continuous verification. AI-powered threat monitoring systems ingest data from endpoints, firewalls, identity systems, cloud logs, application activity, and network traffic, then build a living map of what "normal" looks like for every user and system. When something deviates from that baseline, AI raises alerts, takes automated action, and learns from the outcome. Security becomes proactive instead of reactive, predictive instead of forensic.

One of the most powerful advantages of AI-driven zero-trust systems is their ability to detect attacks that no one has ever seen before. Traditional cybersecurity depends heavily on known threat signatures and predefined rules. AI does not. Machine learning models identify patterns, relationships, and behaviors that humans would never notice. They can spot subtle lateral movement inside a network, detect credential misuse, recognize abnormal API calls, and flag insider threats that look legitimate on the surface. In a world where AI-generated malware and autonomous hacking tools can evolve every minute, only AI-based defense systems can keep up. Zero-trust architecture provides the structure, and AI provides the intelligence.

This book will take you deep into how zero-trust security is designed, deployed, and enforced using artificial intelligence.

You will learn how identity and access management becomes dynamic instead of static, how micro-segmentation prevents attackers from moving freely, how AI models evaluate risk in real time, and how automated response systems isolate threats before they can spread. You will also explore how organizations protect cloud environments, remote workers, and AI-driven applications using continuous verification and behavioral analysis. These are the systems that protect banks, governments, hospitals, defense contractors, and global enterprises from catastrophic breaches and digital warfare.

Zero-trust is not just about stopping hackers; it is about creating resilience in an era of permanent cyber conflict. No system can be perfectly secure, but zero-trust ensures that when something goes wrong, damage is contained, detected, and neutralized as fast as possible. AI-powered monitoring turns security into a living system that adapts, improves, and grows stronger with every attempted attack. As cyber threats become more automated, more intelligent, and more destructive, organizations that fail to adopt zero-trust architectures will become easy targets for AI-driven cybercrime.

By the end of this book, you will understand how the most advanced security systems in the world use artificial intelligence to continuously watch, evaluate, and defend digital environments. You will see how zero-trust replaces outdated perimeter defenses with intelligent, adaptive protection that works everywhere, at all times, against both human and machine attackers. In the age of artificial intelligence, trust is no longer a feature — it is a vulnerability. Zero-trust security and AI threat monitoring are the only path forward for survival in the digital battlefield.

Chapter 1

The Collapse of Perimeter Security

The era of perimeter-based cybersecurity is over. For decades, organizations protected their digital assets the same way medieval cities protected their walls—by building strong borders and assuming everything inside was safe. Firewalls, VPNs, passwords, and internal networks formed a hardened outer shell that kept attackers out. But artificial intelligence, cloud computing, mobile devices, and remote work have shattered those walls. Today's networks have no clear boundaries. Employees log in from coffee shops, airports, home Wi-Fi networks, and foreign countries. Applications live in dozens of cloud environments. AI systems exchange data across platforms in milliseconds. In this world, there is no longer an "inside" or an "outside," only a constantly shifting digital ecosystem that is either being monitored or being exploited.

Hackers no longer need to break in. They log in. They steal credentials using AI-generated phishing attacks, deepfake phone calls, and automated password cracking. They compromise one device, one account, or one software integration, and from there they move silently through the network. Traditional security tools are blind to this kind of intrusion because nothing looks obviously malicious. The attacker is using real usernames, valid passwords, and legitimate system commands. In a perimeter-based system, once someone is authenticated, they are trusted. That trust becomes the doorway to disaster.

Artificial intelligence has made this problem exponentially worse. AI-powered hacking tools can scan millions of endpoints, test thousands of credentials, and identify weaknesses faster than any human team ever could. They learn from every failed attempt and adjust their strategy in real time. When they get inside, they can map the network, locate sensitive data, and decide exactly how to extract or encrypt it. This means that even the smallest breach can become catastrophic in minutes. The old idea of detecting an attack after it happens is no longer acceptable. Defense must be continuous, intelligent, and automatic.

Zero-trust security was created in response to this reality. It is built on a single, radical idea: never trust, always verify. No user, no device, no application, and no system is ever assumed to be safe, even if it has already been authenticated. Every action must be evaluated in context. Who is making the request? From what device? From what location? At what time? With what behavior history? AI systems analyze all of these signals instantly to determine whether a request is legitimate or suspicious. Access is not a one-time decision. It is a continuous calculation.

Instead of giving users broad access to an entire network, zero-trust systems use micro-segmentation to divide everything into small, isolated zones. A compromised account might be able to access one system but nothing else. Even if an attacker gets in, they cannot move freely. Every attempt to access new data triggers another verification process powered by AI. This creates a digital maze where every step is watched, measured, and potentially blocked.

AI threat monitoring makes zero-trust possible at scale. Humans cannot manually track billions of data points across cloud systems, networks, endpoints, and applications. AI models build behavior profiles for every user and system, learning what “normal” looks like. When behavior changes, such as a user suddenly downloading large amounts of data or accessing systems they have never touched before, the AI flags it instantly. Automated response systems can lock accounts, isolate devices, or require additional authentication before damage occurs.

The collapse of perimeter security is not a future threat; it is already happening. Organizations that still rely on outdated trust models are being breached, extorted, and infiltrated every day. Zero-trust and AI threat monitoring represent a fundamental shift in how security is designed. Instead of defending walls, organizations defend every interaction. Instead of trusting credentials, they trust behavior. Instead of reacting to attacks, they predict and prevent them.

In this new digital battlefield, survival depends on visibility, intelligence, and speed. Zero-trust provides the architecture. AI provides the brain. Together, they create a system that can see everything, question everything, and respond instantly. This is not just a new security model. It is the only model capable of defending modern networks against AI-powered cyber threats.

The Network That Never Slept

The first alert came at 2:17 a.m., when the system noticed a login from a location that didn't exist. The coordinates didn't map to any city, country, or known network. To a human, it would have looked like a harmless glitch. To the AI monitoring the zero-trust system, it was a warning. The account belonged to a senior engineer who normally logged in from California. Now, the system saw a request coming from somewhere that had no physical location at all, a synthetic node created by an AI-powered hacking platform.

The attacker thought they had won. The credentials were valid. The password was correct. The multi-factor token had been intercepted by a deepfake voice system that convinced the engineer's phone to authorize the login. In a traditional network, the hacker would have been inside with full access. But this network didn't trust anyone, not even its own employees. The AI instantly began watching every move.

The hacker tried to access the customer database. The AI noticed the engineer had never accessed that system before. The risk score increased. The attacker attempted to download files. The speed and volume were far above the engineer's normal behavior. The AI quietly restricted access without alerting the intruder. From the hacker's perspective, the system simply slowed down.

Frustrated, the attacker moved laterally, trying to reach a financial server. Again, the zero-trust system blocked the request. Each attempt made the attacker more visible, more suspicious, more exposed. The AI compared thousands of variables, device fingerprints, command patterns, timing intervals, and historical data. Within seconds, it was certain this was not the real engineer.

Without any human intervention, the AI isolated the session. The compromised credentials were locked. The attacker's connection was cut off. Forensics systems began tracing the origin of the intrusion while backup AI agents verified that no data had been touched. By the time the sun rose, the attack was already over.

The engineer woke up to a notification explaining that an attempted breach had been stopped overnight. He never lost a file. No customers were affected. No systems went down. The network had defended itself while everyone slept.

That was the power of zero-trust combined with AI threat monitoring. The system didn't wait for alarms. It didn't wait for damage. It watched every action, questioned every request, and shut down danger before it could become disaster. In a world of AI-driven cyber warfare, the safest networks are the ones that never close their eyes.

Chapter 2

How AI Sees Threats Humans Can't

Artificial intelligence has fundamentally changed how cybersecurity works because it sees patterns where humans only see noise. Traditional security tools rely on predefined rules, static threat signatures, and manual investigation. They are built to recognize what is already known. AI, by contrast, is designed to learn. It builds mathematical models of behavior across millions of data points, continuously refining what "normal" looks like for every user, device, and application. In a zero-trust environment, this ability becomes the nervous system of the network, constantly sensing subtle signals that something is wrong long before a breach becomes visible.

Every action on a digital system leaves a trail of data. Logins, keystrokes, file access, API calls, network packets, cloud events, and application activity all form behavioral fingerprints. Humans cannot process this level of complexity, but AI thrives on it. Machine learning systems compare real-time activity against historical baselines, identifying micro-anomalies that indicate compromise. A login that occurs three minutes earlier than usual, a data query that runs slightly faster than normal, or a command sequence that is out of order may seem insignificant alone, but together they form a threat signature that only AI can recognize.

In zero-trust environments, AI does not ask whether credentials are correct. It asks whether the behavior makes sense. A valid password does not mean a legitimate user. If a trusted account suddenly starts accessing systems it never touched before, transferring files at unusual speeds, or operating from an unfamiliar device, the AI assigns risk instantly. The more anomalies it detects, the higher the risk score becomes. When the risk crosses a threshold, access is restricted, challenged, or terminated automatically. No human needs to review a log or approve a response. The system acts in real time, stopping attacks before they escalate.

One of the most dangerous threats in modern cybersecurity is the insider attack. This can be a malicious employee, a compromised account, or an AI-driven impersonation. Traditional security models struggle here because the attacker appears legitimate. AI excels at detecting insiders because it does not rely on identity alone. It relies on patterns of behavior. Every person has a digital rhythm, the way they move through systems, the timing of their work, the types of files they access, and the commands they use. When that rhythm changes, the AI notices immediately. AI also monitors machines and software the same way it monitors people. Servers, applications, APIs, and AI agents all have behavioral profiles. When malware infects a system, it changes how that system behaves. It may start making new network connections, executing unfamiliar commands, or transmitting unusual data. AI models flag these deviations even when the malware itself is unknown. This allows zero-trust systems to detect zero-day attacks that have never been seen before, closing the gap between exploitation and response.

Threat monitoring powered by AI also creates predictive security. Instead of waiting for attacks to happen, machine learning models identify vulnerabilities and risky patterns before they are exploited. If certain types of logins or software configurations are frequently associated with breaches, the AI raises alerts and strengthens defenses automatically. This turns cybersecurity from a reactive process into a proactive one, where risks are reduced before damage occurs.

The speed of AI is what makes this possible. Attacks now unfold in seconds, not days. AI threat monitoring evaluates thousands of signals for every request, calculating risk in real time. This allows zero-trust systems to make access decisions instantly, balancing security and usability without human bottlenecks. Users experience seamless access when their behavior is normal, and invisible barriers when something is wrong. As cyber threats become more intelligent, more automated, and more adaptive, human-driven security operations cannot keep up. AI becomes the only viable defender, watching everything, learning continuously, and acting without hesitation. In a zero-trust world, AI is not just a tool. It is the guardian of every digital interaction.

The Pattern No One Could See

No one at the company noticed anything unusual at first. The numbers were right. The logins were valid. The systems were running smoothly. But the AI did notice. It saw that one employee, a data analyst named Michael, had started working differently. His login times were slightly off. His data queries were more complex than usual. His file downloads were faster. None of it was dramatic, but together it formed a pattern that didn't belong to Michael.

The truth was that Michael's laptop had been compromised by an AI-powered malware agent. It silently watched everything he did, copied his credentials, and began using his access to explore the company's systems. The malware moved carefully, mimicking Michael's behavior just enough to avoid detection by traditional security tools. To humans, everything looked normal.

But the zero-trust AI saw the differences. It noticed that Michael's account was accessing databases he had never used before. It detected subtle changes in command sequences and timing. It watched as the malware began preparing to extract sensitive data. The risk score climbed quietly, crossing the threshold where action was required.

Without warning the attacker, the system restricted Michael's account to a limited sandbox. The malware tried to move laterally to another server and was blocked. It attempted to exfiltrate data and was cut off. Confused, it tried again, revealing even more anomalies. Each move made it more visible.

Within seconds, the AI isolated the infected laptop and alerted security. Michael was contacted and asked to reboot his device. The malware was removed before any data was lost. The attacker never even realized how close they had come.

Michael returned to work the next day unaware that a silent war had been fought on his behalf. The zero-trust system had watched, learned, and acted without human intervention. It had seen a pattern no one else could see, and it had saved the company without anyone ever knowing how close disaster had been.

Chapter 3

Identity, Devices, and Continuous Verification

In a zero-trust world, identity is no longer a single moment of authentication but a living, evolving profile that is constantly verified. Traditional security systems treat identity as something you prove once, usually with a password, a token, or a biometric scan. Once verified, you are trusted until you log out. That model collapses under modern cyber threats, especially in environments filled with cloud applications, mobile devices, remote workers, and artificial intelligence systems that act on behalf of humans. Zero-trust replaces static identity with continuous verification, where AI monitors not just who you are, but how you behave, what device you are using, where you are connecting from, and whether every action makes sense in context.

Every digital identity today is a composite of many signals. A user is not just a username and password. They are a device fingerprint, an IP address, a geolocation pattern, a browser profile, a typing rhythm, an application usage history, and a behavioral baseline. AI systems stitch these signals together into an identity fabric that is far harder to fake than credentials alone. When someone logs in, the AI evaluates all of these factors instantly. A correct password from an unfamiliar device in an unusual location at an odd time of day creates a very different risk profile than the same password from a known laptop in a normal working environment.

Devices themselves become identities in a zero-trust architecture. Every phone, laptop, server, IoT device, and cloud workload has its own behavioral fingerprint. AI models track how each device communicates, what software it runs, how often it connects, and what data it accesses. When malware infects a device, its behavior changes. It may start sending data to unknown servers, executing unfamiliar processes, or scanning internal networks. Even if the attacker has valid credentials, the compromised device exposes itself through these subtle changes. Zero-trust systems can isolate or restrict that device before it becomes a launchpad for further attacks.

Continuous verification means that authentication never truly ends. AI does not simply validate identity at login; it reassesses trust every second. If a user logs in from a trusted laptop but then suddenly starts issuing commands that do not match their role, the AI raises their risk score. If they attempt to access sensitive systems they have never touched before, additional verification may be required. If the behavior looks dangerous, access can be revoked instantly. This dynamic trust model makes it nearly impossible for attackers to hide behind stolen credentials.

This approach also protects against one of the most dangerous modern threats: AI-powered impersonation. Deepfake voices, synthetic video, and AI-generated text can convincingly imitate real people. A hacker may trick an employee into approving a login or sharing a token. In a zero-trust environment, that approval alone is not enough. The AI compares the behavior of the session against the real user's historical patterns. If something does not match, the system intervenes. Identity becomes something that must be proven continuously, not something that can be stolen once.

Cloud computing and AI automation make this even more critical. Many actions today are performed by software agents, APIs, and autonomous systems. These digital entities must also be verified and monitored. Zero-trust AI systems assign identities to these non-human actors, tracking how they behave and what they are allowed to do. If an AI agent starts acting outside its normal scope, such as accessing financial records or exporting large amounts of data, the system flags and restricts it just like a human user.

The result of continuous identity and device verification is a security model that adapts in real time. Trust is no longer binary. It is a fluid score that changes with every action. AI makes this possible by processing enormous amounts of data instantly and making nuanced decisions that balance security and productivity. Users experience smooth access when their behavior is normal and friction only when something looks wrong. Attackers, by contrast, are constantly challenged, slowed, and ultimately exposed.

In the age of artificial intelligence, identity is the new perimeter. Zero-trust security wraps that identity in layers of continuous verification that no static credential can bypass. With AI watching every interaction, every device, and every behavioral shift, the digital world becomes a place where trust must be earned again and again, moment by moment.

The Face That Wasn't Hers

The call came in with Maria's voice. It sounded exactly like her, calm and professional, asking the IT team to approve an urgent access request. In the past, that would have been enough. Maria was the chief financial officer. Her word carried weight. But this company no longer trusted voices alone.

The AI system analyzed the request as it came in. The tone matched Maria's voice, but the timing was wrong. She was usually in meetings at that hour. The device making the request was new. The IP address was from a country she had never visited. Individually, none of it would have raised alarm. Together, it formed a risk profile that could not be ignored.

Behind the scenes, a deepfake engine was generating Maria's voice in real time, trying to trick the system into approving access to the company's financial servers. The attacker believed they had cracked the hardest part, identity. But the zero-trust AI was already questioning everything.

When the request was approved for limited access, the attacker tried to move quickly, opening financial records and initiating transfers. The AI compared the behavior to Maria's normal patterns. She never worked that fast. She never accessed those files in that order. The risk score spiked.

Without any alert to the attacker, the system silently restricted access. Every command was routed into a secure sandbox. The attacker kept trying, growing more aggressive, revealing more anomalies with every move. Within seconds, the session was isolated and terminated.

Maria was still in her meeting when she received a message that someone had tried to become her. Nothing was stolen. Nothing was changed. The system had protected her identity better than any password ever could.

In a world where faces and voices could be faked, it was

behavior that told the truth. The zero-trust AI had seen through the illusion and stopped the attack before it even began.

Chapter 4

Micro-Segmentation, Lateral Movement & AI Containment

One of the greatest weaknesses of traditional networks is not how attackers get in, but how freely they move once they do. In legacy security models, a single compromised account or device can often access vast portions of the internal network. This allows hackers to explore, escalate privileges, locate valuable data, and deploy malware across multiple systems. In the age of AI-powered cyber attacks, this freedom of movement turns small breaches into full-scale disasters. Zero-trust security solves this problem through micro-segmentation, an architecture that breaks the network into tightly controlled zones that are continuously monitored and enforced by artificial intelligence.

Micro-segmentation means that every application, database, server, user group, and device exists in its own security boundary. Instead of a flat network where everything is connected, the environment becomes a collection of isolated compartments. Even if an attacker gains access to one segment, they cannot automatically reach anything else. Each attempt to move from one zone to another is treated as a new access request, evaluated by AI in real time. This creates a digital maze where every step is watched, verified, and potentially blocked.

Lateral movement is the primary goal of most cyber intrusions. Once inside a network, attackers try to jump from system to system, hunting for credentials, sensitive data, or control over critical infrastructure. AI-powered malware is especially good at this. It maps networks, tests permissions, and adapts its strategy based on what it discovers. Micro-segmentation turns this advantage into a liability. Every move exposes the attacker to new checks, new risk evaluations, and new opportunities for detection.

AI threat monitoring is what makes micro-segmentation effective. The system does not just block everything by default; it understands how legitimate traffic should flow between segments. Machine learning models build profiles of how applications communicate, how users access resources, and how data normally moves. When something deviates from these patterns, the AI flags it immediately. An application that suddenly starts querying a financial database, or a user account that tries to access server infrastructure, triggers an automated response. This prevents attackers from blending into the background as they move.

Containment is the ultimate goal. In a zero-trust architecture, breaches are expected, but disasters are not. When AI detects suspicious lateral movement, it can isolate a single device, account, or application without shutting down the entire organization. The affected segment is locked, traffic is rerouted, and forensic systems begin analyzing what happened. This limits the blast radius of an attack, turning what could have been a company-wide crisis into a minor, manageable incident.

This approach is especially critical in cloud and AI-driven environments, where systems are highly interconnected. APIs talk to other APIs. AI agents pull data from multiple sources. Automation pipelines move information across platforms. Micro-segmentation ensures that these connections exist only where they are needed and only when they are behaving as expected. If an AI agent is compromised, it cannot suddenly access payroll systems or customer databases because those pathways are closed by design.

AI containment also allows organizations to fight back intelligently. When suspicious activity is detected, the system can quietly observe the attacker, learning their methods and intentions before cutting them off. This intelligence is used to strengthen defenses across the entire network. Every blocked movement, every failed access request, and every isolated segment becomes training data for the AI, making future attacks even harder. The combination of micro-segmentation and AI-driven containment transforms cybersecurity from a brittle defense into a resilient, adaptive system. Instead of collapsing when breached, the network absorbs the impact, limits the damage, and learns from the experience. In a world of automated cyber warfare, this ability to contain and adapt is what separates survivable incidents from existential threats.

The Maze the Hacker Couldn't Escape

The attacker thought the first server was the hard part. Once inside, everything should have been open. That was how it always worked. But this network felt different. Every time the hacker tried to move, something slowed them down.

They started on a web server and tried to jump to the internal database. Access denied. They tried another system. Blocked. The malware running the attack mapped the network, looking for a path forward, but every door required a new set of credentials, a new identity check, a new behavioral validation.

The AI was watching quietly. It saw the repeated access attempts, the unusual sequence of requests, the probing behavior that no legitimate application would ever perform. The risk score climbed, but the system didn't immediately shut the attacker out. It wanted to learn.

The hacker finally found a narrow pathway into a less protected segment, a small service used for data processing. They celebrated too early. That segment was isolated from everything valuable. When they tried to move again, they were trapped.

Behind the scenes, the AI locked down the compromised server. It mirrored the attacker's activity, capturing every command and every packet. When the attacker tried to deploy ransomware, it was contained inside the segment, unable to spread.

Minutes later, the connection was terminated. The attack was over. No data was stolen. No systems were encrypted. The company never even noticed.

To the hacker, the network felt like a labyrinth with no exit. To the zero-trust AI, it was just another test, another opportunity to learn, and another threat quietly neutralized.

Chapter 5

Real-Time AI Risk Scoring & Automated Response

Zero-trust security cannot function without real-time risk intelligence. In a modern digital environment, millions of access requests, file transfers, API calls, and system actions occur every second. Treating all of them equally is impossible. What makes zero-trust effective is its ability to evaluate every action based on risk, using artificial intelligence to calculate whether something is safe, suspicious, or dangerous. AI risk scoring turns security into a living system that continuously measures the likelihood of compromise and responds instantly when that risk becomes unacceptable.

Every digital interaction carries risk. A user logging in from a familiar device during normal business hours is low risk. The same user logging in from a new device in a foreign country at 3 a.m. is higher risk. AI models analyze thousands of variables including identity, device health, location, behavior history, application sensitivity, network conditions, and threat intelligence. These variables are combined into a real-time risk score that determines how much access should be granted. Instead of relying on rigid rules, the system makes nuanced decisions based on context.

As risk increases, zero-trust systems automatically change how access works. Low-risk activity is seamless and fast. Medium-risk activity may trigger additional verification such as multi-factor authentication or step-up identity checks. High-risk activity may result in restricted access, session isolation, or immediate termination. This allows organizations to remain productive without sacrificing security. Users are only challenged when something is genuinely unusual.

Automated response is the other half of this equation. In the age of AI-powered attacks, there is no time to wait for human approval. When a threat emerges, the system must act instantly. AI-driven response engines can lock accounts, block network traffic, isolate devices, revoke tokens, and contain compromised systems in seconds. These actions happen silently and precisely, targeting only what is necessary while leaving the rest of the organization unaffected.

One of the most powerful advantages of AI risk scoring is its ability to adapt. The models learn from every incident, every false alarm, and every confirmed attack. Over time, they become better at distinguishing between harmless anomalies and real threats. This reduces alert fatigue for security teams and improves the accuracy of automated decisions. The system evolves with the threat landscape, always refining its understanding of risk. Real-time risk scoring also enables predictive defense. AI models recognize patterns that often precede attacks, such as unusual login attempts, changes in application behavior, or spikes in data access. When these patterns appear, the system can raise defenses before an attack fully unfolds. This shifts cybersecurity from a reactive discipline to a proactive one, where many threats are neutralized before they ever become breaches.

In a zero-trust architecture, every action is a decision, and every decision is informed by AI. Trust is no longer static. It is recalculated continuously. This creates a dynamic security environment that can withstand even the most sophisticated AI-driven threats.

The Score That Saved the Company

The system noticed the anomaly before anyone else did. A user named Daniel logged in from his office laptop, just as he did every morning. At first, the risk score was low. But then Daniel's account attempted to access a cloud server he had never touched before. The risk score ticked upward.

Seconds later, large data queries began. Daniel usually worked with reports, not raw databases. The AI compared this behavior to his historical profile. The mismatch was growing. The risk score climbed again. Unknown to Daniel, his laptop had been infected by a remote access trojan controlled by an

AI-powered hacking platform. The attacker was moving carefully, using Daniel's identity to avoid detection. But the zero-trust system was not fooled by credentials alone.

When the malware tried to export customer records, the risk score crossed the critical threshold. Instantly, the AI isolated Daniel's session. The data transfer was blocked. His account was locked. The laptop was placed in quarantine. All of this happened in less than a second.

Daniel was confused when his screen went dark, but the company was safe. Security teams were alerted, the malware was removed, and no data was lost.

The attacker never got a second chance. In a world where cyber threats move at machine speed, it was the AI's ability to calculate risk and act instantly that made all the difference.

Chapter 6

Behavioral Analytics, Threat Patterns, and Adaptive AI Response

In a world where cyberattacks are increasingly intelligent, the ability to detect subtle deviations from normal behavior is critical. Traditional security measures rely heavily on signatures, rules, or static thresholds. These approaches work for known threats but fail to detect the unknown, the zero-day exploits, and the AI-driven attacks that can adapt to existing defenses. Behavioral analytics, powered by AI, forms the cornerstone of modern zero-trust systems. By continuously analyzing user and system behavior, AI identifies patterns that indicate malicious activity even when no known threat signatures exist.

Behavioral analytics begins with the collection of data. Every login, file access, system command, API request, and network transaction generates signals. Each user leaves a unique digital footprint: patterns of activity that are highly individual. AI models ingest this data to establish a baseline for what constitutes normal behavior. This baseline is not static; it evolves with the user's habits, seasonal workflows, system updates, and environmental factors. By continuously learning, the AI creates a living profile for every user, device, application, and network node.

Once baselines are established, AI detects anomalies in real time. An unusual login from an unexpected location, data access outside of standard workflows, or abnormal application behavior triggers immediate scrutiny. Unlike static rules, AI evaluates context: is the user acting differently because of a legitimate reason, such as a travel schedule, or is this behavior indicative of compromise? By correlating multiple signals, AI determines risk scores that guide automated responses within a zero-trust framework. The system can escalate, restrict, or monitor activity without human intervention, ensuring the balance between security and productivity.

AI-driven behavioral analytics also addresses the challenge of lateral movement. Once attackers breach a network, they often attempt to move horizontally, probing for vulnerabilities, escalating privileges, and seeking high-value assets. Each lateral move generates subtle deviations from established patterns. AI systems map the relationships between users, devices, and systems, allowing them to detect when an entity is moving in ways that are inconsistent with its typical behavior. This enables early containment, preventing attackers from reaching sensitive data or critical infrastructure. Adaptive response is a natural extension of behavioral analytics. When AI detects abnormal behavior, it can respond automatically, scaling its actions based on severity. For low-risk deviations, the system may simply monitor the activity more closely. For medium-risk events, additional authentication steps or device verification may be enforced. High-risk events trigger immediate isolation of accounts or devices, network segmentation, and forensic investigation. This tiered approach ensures that threats are contained efficiently, without unnecessary disruption to legitimate activity.

Behavioral analytics also enhances predictive security. By analyzing trends, correlations, and historical incidents, AI can identify emerging threat patterns. For example, a series of minor anomalies across multiple user accounts may indicate a coordinated attack. The system can adjust its thresholds, implement proactive defenses, and alert security teams to prepare for targeted campaigns. This transforms security from reactive incident management into proactive threat prevention.

One of the most powerful applications of behavioral analytics is in detecting AI-driven social engineering attacks. Phishing, spear-phishing, and impersonation attempts are increasingly crafted using AI to mimic legitimate users, voices, or communications. Behavioral analytics does not rely on the content alone. Instead, it evaluates whether the actions associated with the communication align with historical patterns. If an email requests unusual system access or a message attempts to redirect funds in a way that deviates from normal behavior, AI identifies it immediately and initiates containment measures.

The combination of behavioral analytics, threat pattern recognition, and adaptive AI response creates a security environment that is always learning, always vigilant, and always responsive. It enables organizations to detect the undetectable, respond at machine speed, and evolve with the threat landscape. In a zero-trust architecture, AI becomes the sentinel that never sleeps, the analyst that never tires, and the decision-maker that acts instantly when risk is detected. It is no longer sufficient to simply block known threats; modern cybersecurity requires systems that understand behavior, anticipate attacks, and react autonomously, ensuring that networks remain resilient in the age of AI-powered threats.

The Algorithm That Knew Too Much

It was a quiet Monday morning when the security operations center received the first alert. To the human eye, nothing appeared unusual. A routine login had occurred on one of the cloud servers. The employee, named Elena, had accessed the database dozens of times before. Her credentials were valid, her device recognized. But the AI observed subtle deviations. Elena's activity was slightly faster, her queries were more complex, and the endpoints she accessed were not typical for her role.

The AI began analyzing the context. Was Elena working remotely from a coffee shop, or was this a compromised session? Her geolocation was consistent with her home city, but the IP address belonged to an unusual range associated with recent attack attempts. The AI's behavioral model instantly compared these actions with historical patterns, analyzing timing, keystrokes, device fingerprints, and data access behavior. A risk score began to climb.

Minutes later, the anomaly expanded. Elena's account, now under AI observation, attempted to export multiple financial spreadsheets and access archived payroll files she had never touched before. Each action alone was subtle, almost imperceptible. Combined, they painted a pattern that the AI recognized as suspicious. The risk score reached a critical threshold, triggering an adaptive response.

The AI immediately restricted Elena's account, allowing only read-only access to non-critical data while isolating her session. Simultaneously, the system flagged all associated endpoints, tracing connections and monitoring traffic in real time. It created a shadow map of the attempted activity, capturing every request the attacker tried to make through

Elena's compromised credentials. Behind the scenes, the attacker—an AI-driven malware agent—had infiltrated the company's network using a sophisticated spear-phishing campaign. It had learned Elena's email patterns and mimicked her communication style to obtain access. But the AI's behavioral analytics had caught deviations too small for humans to notice. The malware's attempts to move laterally triggered alerts at every step.

The AI escalated its response. Network segmentation tools were deployed automatically, containing the affected subnetwork. Any attempts to reach sensitive financial servers were blocked. Forensics logs began capturing every byte of traffic, every command executed, and every endpoint interaction. The malware adapted, changing tactics, rerouting requests, attempting to bypass the AI's detection. Each adaptation, however, left new patterns for the AI to analyze, refine, and counteract.

Over the next thirty minutes, the AI effectively engaged in a silent duel with the malware. It monitored, predicted, and responded to every move, preventing lateral movement, halting data exfiltration, and isolating every suspicious process. By the time the human security team arrived, the attack had been contained. Elena's session was restored after a secure device verification. No files were lost, no data leaked, and the malware had been neutralized within its quarantined environment.

Elena never realized the scale of the attack. She simply received a notification explaining that unusual activity had been detected and her session had been temporarily restricted. The company, however, had been defended by an algorithm that could see patterns no human could detect, understand subtle behavioral deviations, and respond in real time.

Later, the security team would review the AI's logs and marvel at its sophistication. Every action by the malware had been predicted, countered, and contained. The system had learned from the attack, refining its behavioral models to prevent similar incidents in the future.

In the world of AI-driven cyber threats, the safest networks were those that never slept, never assumed trust, and always analyzed behavior. That day, the AI had proven itself not just a tool, but a guardian—adaptive, intelligent, and relentless.

Chapter 7

AI-Driven Threat Hunting & Autonomous Containment

In the modern cybersecurity landscape, breaches are no longer a matter of if, but when. Organizations that rely solely on passive defense are constantly at risk. Zero-trust security combined with AI-driven threat hunting transforms this paradigm by making detection, analysis, and containment proactive and continuous. Rather than waiting for alerts generated by traditional signature-based systems, AI continuously scours networks, endpoints, cloud applications, and user activity to identify subtle indicators of compromise. The system actively searches for patterns that suggest unauthorized access, data exfiltration, malware deployment, or AI-powered attacks, ensuring threats are discovered and mitigated before they can escalate.

AI-driven threat hunting begins with behavioral baselining. Every user, device, application, and network node has an established pattern of activity. AI analyzes login times, data access patterns, command sequences, API calls, and network traffic to define normal operations. These baselines are dynamic, adapting as users' behaviors change, as systems update, and as new applications are introduced. When deviations occur—no matter how small—they are flagged for further analysis. Unlike human analysts, AI can continuously monitor millions of actions in real time, identifying anomalies that might otherwise go unnoticed for hours, days, or even weeks.

Once a potential threat is identified, autonomous containment mechanisms activate immediately. Isolation is performed at granular levels: an endpoint may be quarantined, a user session temporarily restricted, or a cloud application segmented from the rest of the network. The AI can enforce micro-segmentation dynamically, ensuring that lateral movement by attackers is prevented while normal operations continue. This containment is automated, precise, and fast, often neutralizing threats in seconds, far faster than human teams could respond.

The intelligence gathered by AI during threat hunting is invaluable. Every anomalous activity, every attempted breach, and every malicious signature feeds machine learning models, refining their predictive capability. AI identifies not only the specific attack but also related patterns that indicate coordinated campaigns. It can detect low-and-slow intrusions, insider threats, and AI-assisted social engineering attempts that humans could easily overlook. This continuous learning loop strengthens security over time, making the system more resilient and adaptive with each encounter. Integration across multiple platforms is critical. AI threat hunting spans endpoints, servers, cloud environments, SaaS applications, IoT devices, and AI agents themselves. It monitors communications, interactions, and dependencies, creating a comprehensive map of the digital ecosystem. Any unexpected connection, unusual data flow, or abnormal process triggers investigation and, if necessary, immediate containment. In effect, the AI becomes both scout and guard, identifying emerging threats while simultaneously deploying defense measures.

Autonomous containment also minimizes organizational disruption. Traditional incident response often requires manual intervention, taking systems offline and causing downtime. AI systems can isolate only the affected components, maintain business continuity, and provide actionable intelligence for security teams. This ensures that operations continue uninterrupted while attackers are blocked from advancing.

The combination of AI-driven threat hunting and autonomous containment represents a significant evolution in zero-trust security. No longer is cybersecurity reactive or dependent on human speed and memory. AI enables continuous monitoring, instant analysis, rapid decision-making, and precise intervention. Organizations are no longer waiting to detect a breach—they are actively hunting threats, containing them automatically, and learning from every incident. In the era of AI-powered attacks, this proactive, autonomous, adaptive approach is not just an advantage—it is a necessity.

The Intruder Who Never Arrived

It was the middle of the night when the first unusual activity appeared. An AI-powered malware agent had infiltrated the network through a compromised contractor account. The attacker's goal was to extract sensitive financial data and install ransomware across the cloud servers. To a human security team, the network looked normal. All logins were valid. All applications responded as expected. No alarms had been triggered. But the zero-trust AI was already aware.

The AI noticed micro-anomalies immediately. The contractor account accessed systems that it had never touched before, issuing commands in a sequence slightly out of order. The AI correlated the activity with geolocation, device signatures, and past behavior. The risk score started climbing. Within seconds, the AI had isolated the account into a quarantined segment, preventing the malware from reaching critical infrastructure.

The attacker attempted lateral movement, hopping to adjacent servers. Each time, the AI detected abnormal communication patterns. Traffic that appeared legitimate to conventional monitoring was flagged as inconsistent with expected behavior. The malware tried to mimic normal user activity, slowing its requests, spreading its access over multiple endpoints, but every subtle deviation was recorded. The AI adjusted containment measures dynamically, creating virtual firewalls around the compromised segments, effectively constructing a digital maze the intruder could not navigate.

Meanwhile, autonomous forensics initiated. The AI began analyzing every packet of data, mapping the malware's intended path, and predicting its next moves. The system recognized patterns consistent with a previous campaign of AI-driven attacks on a competitor. Learning from prior incidents, the AI anticipated the malware's strategy, blocking key communications and preventing any data exfiltration attempts. The malware was trapped within its isolated zone, unable to propagate.

The attacker, believing they had successfully breached the network, attempted a bold move. They tried to escalate privileges, hoping to gain administrative access. The AI responded instantaneously, cutting off permission elevation, logging every failed attempt, and alerting the human security team. By the time anyone was awake, the breach had already been neutralized. No files had been copied, no systems encrypted, and the attacker had gained nothing.

Over the next hours, the AI continued to monitor. It detected residual scripts left by the malware, automatically removing them and restoring the network to a clean state. It reinforced micro-segmentation policies, recalibrated behavioral baselines, and adjusted risk scoring thresholds based on the lessons learned from the attempted attack. Every move by the AI improved its understanding of future threats.

The security team reviewed the incident later that morning. They marveled at the detailed logs, the precision of containment, and the speed of neutralization. The malware had been active for only a brief period, yet it had accomplished nothing. The AI had acted faster than any human could have, predicted the attack's movements, and neutralized the threat autonomously.

Elena, the CTO, reflected on the incident. The network had been breached in theory, but in practice, the intruder had never arrived. Every attempt had been anticipated, contained, and analyzed in real time. The zero-trust AI had functioned as scout, analyst, and defender simultaneously. It had learned from the attack, strengthened defenses, and ensured the safety of every system and every user.

By noon, operations continued as usual, unaware of how close disaster had come. The AI had proven its value, not just as a passive monitor, but as an active hunter and autonomous guardian. The intruder would try again someday, but the network was ready. It never slept. It never trusted. And it never failed.

Chapter 8

Continuous Learning, Threat Intelligence, and Future-Proof Zero-Trust

The cybersecurity battlefield is constantly evolving. Threats that were unthinkable yesterday become routine today, and tomorrow's attacks are likely to be far more sophisticated, automated, and AI-driven. Zero-trust security is not a static system—it is dynamic, adaptive, and continuously learning. At the heart of this evolution is the combination of real-time threat intelligence, machine learning, and AI-driven behavioral analysis. Continuous learning ensures that defenses do not remain fixed, but instead evolve as threats evolve, creating a proactive rather than reactive security posture.

Continuous learning begins with the integration of threat intelligence feeds. AI systems ingest data from multiple sources, including global cybersecurity databases, dark web monitoring, malware signatures, and reports of emerging attack vectors. This data is analyzed in real time to identify patterns, correlations, and predictive indicators. The AI not only notes known threats but also recognizes precursors—behavioral anomalies and network activities that often precede attacks. By combining global threat intelligence with internal behavioral analytics, zero-trust systems create a multi-layered understanding of risk across the entire digital environment.

Machine learning models continuously analyze user, device, and system activity to update behavioral baselines. Every login, data access, API call, and network transaction contributes to the AI's understanding of normal operations. As workflows change, as employees move, as cloud services are added, and as AI agents perform automated tasks, the system adapts. This ensures that what is considered "normal" remains relevant, and that anomalies can be detected with precision, reducing false positives while maintaining high sensitivity to genuine threats.

Adaptive AI response is central to this process. When the system detects unusual behavior—whether from a human user, a device, or a software agent—it immediately calculates risk based on context, history, and threat intelligence. Responses are proportionate and precise: a suspicious login may trigger multi-factor verification, while abnormal API activity may result in session isolation. More severe events activate autonomous containment, micro-segmentation, and forensic capture. The AI effectively learns not only from each incident but also from the outcomes of its own actions, continuously refining its decision-making process. Collaboration between AI systems and human analysts enhances learning further. Security operations teams can review AI-generated alerts and incident responses, providing feedback that is incorporated into model updates. This human-in-the-loop approach ensures that machine intelligence benefits from domain expertise while freeing humans from the burden of routine monitoring. Over time, the AI becomes increasingly capable of identifying subtle indicators of compromise and predicting attack strategies that no single human could detect.

Threat intelligence is enriched by analyzing patterns across multiple organizations. Shared insights about emerging malware, ransomware tactics, AI-driven social engineering, and zero-day vulnerabilities allow the system to anticipate attacks before they occur within a particular network. When combined with internal monitoring, AI can recognize coordinated campaigns, detect lateral movement attempts, and even predict where an attacker is likely to strike next. This predictive capability is a major differentiator of modern zero-trust architectures.

The future of zero-trust security relies on autonomous adaptation. Networks will continue to grow in complexity, AI attacks will become more sophisticated, and human teams alone will be unable to respond fast enough. Continuous learning ensures that defenses are always evolving, capable of anticipating and countering threats in real time. Organizations that embrace AI-driven adaptive security create resilient digital ecosystems where risk is managed dynamically, trust is never assumed, and the system improves with every encounter.

Ultimately, continuous learning transforms cybersecurity from a reactive function into an intelligent, proactive discipline. Zero-trust architectures, empowered by AI, do more than respond—they predict, contain, and evolve. They create a network that not only survives attacks but becomes stronger because of them. The digital future demands no less. In this environment, only systems that learn, adapt, and act autonomously will remain secure, creating a foundation for resilience in an era dominated by AI-powered threats.

The Network That Learned Too Fast

It started with a minor anomaly: a login from an unfamiliar location that triggered no alerts in traditional systems. The user, Jason, had traveled to another state, but the AI saw the pattern differently. The login coincided with unusual API requests and a sudden increase in data downloads. The system calculated a risk score based on location, device signature, and behavioral deviation. The score was high enough to trigger monitoring but not isolation.

Minutes later, additional anomalies appeared. Another employee's credentials were used to access a different server in a pattern the AI had never seen. The AI connected the two events, analyzing historical baselines, network traffic, and global threat intelligence feeds. The system recognized the hallmarks of an AI-assisted attack that had been detected in other organizations a week earlier. Autonomous containment measures were deployed on the affected endpoints, isolating them without disrupting the broader network.

The malware behind the attack was sophisticated. It mimicked normal user behavior, slowing its queries and randomizing its commands to evade detection. But the AI's continuous learning capabilities allowed it to detect subtle deviations—tiny shifts in timing, anomalies in API call sequences, and unusual file access patterns. It calculated risk scores dynamically, escalating responses as the malware adapted. Each failed attempt to move laterally was logged and used to refine the AI's predictive model.

As the attack progressed, the AI began anticipating the malware's next move. It deployed virtual barriers, segmenting the network preemptively to cut off paths the malware might use. Suspicious processes were quarantined, while legitimate users continued their work uninterrupted. The AI had effectively created a living defense mechanism that learned from the attacker in real time. The malware attempted a bold escalation, trying to access the financial server directly from an isolated segment. The AI had predicted this exact move, preloaded containment protocols, and blocked the attempt instantly. The intruder became trapped in a quarantined zone, unable to communicate with any other part of the network. Every action it took was captured, analyzed, and added to the AI's knowledge base.

By the time the human security team logged in, the attack had already been neutralized. They reviewed the incident and were stunned at the AI's precision. Not only had it contained the malware, but it had also learned from every failed maneuver, updating behavioral baselines, adjusting risk thresholds, and improving predictive defenses. The system was now stronger and faster than it had been moments before the attack began.

Jason returned to work, unaware that his account had been a target. The network continued operating smoothly, data remained secure, and normal operations went uninterrupted. Meanwhile, the AI continued to scan, learn, and adapt, ready for the next threat. It had demonstrated a level of proactive defense that humans could not match, continuously improving itself with each encounter.

Over the following days, the AI analyzed trends, correlated

global threat intelligence, and refined its predictive models. Minor anomalies that would have been ignored before were now flagged automatically, contained, and logged. The network had transformed into a resilient, self-improving ecosystem. Every attempted breach, every subtle deviation, and every attack vector became part of its growing intelligence.

By the end of the week, the human security team marveled at the system's autonomy. The AI had acted faster than any operator could, predicted behaviors, and contained threats without a single human intervention. They realized the network had learned too fast, adapting to threats in real time, outpacing any potential attacker. In a world of AI-powered cybercrime, this learning network had become not just a defender, but a predator: one step ahead, always vigilant, and continually evolving.

Chapter 9

Incident Response, Forensics, and Continuous Improvement

Even the most sophisticated zero-trust security systems are not immune to attacks. Cyber adversaries are increasingly intelligent, automated, and adaptive. While AI-driven threat monitoring, behavioral analytics, and autonomous containment provide strong defenses, breaches or attempted intrusions can still occur. Chapter 9 focuses on the next critical layer of modern zero-trust architecture: incident response, forensic investigation, and continuous improvement. By combining AI with human oversight, organizations can not only neutralize threats but also learn from every encounter, refining defenses and preventing future incidents.

Incident response begins the moment an anomaly is detected or a risk threshold is crossed. In zero-trust environments, AI automatically triggers a tiered response, isolating affected accounts, devices, or network segments while alerting security teams. The speed of response is critical; attacks now move at machine speed, and delays can result in significant damage. AI containment measures act within milliseconds, quarantining suspicious endpoints, restricting sessions, and stopping unauthorized data transfers before human intervention is necessary. This automated triage buys crucial time for analysts to focus on strategic decision-making.

Forensic investigation is the process of understanding what occurred, how it occurred, and what vulnerabilities were exploited. AI accelerates this process by capturing detailed logs, reconstructing attack paths, and mapping interactions across the entire digital ecosystem. Every command, file access, network packet, and process execution is analyzed and correlated. Analysts can use these insights to determine whether an incident was an isolated attempt, part of a coordinated campaign, or the work of AI-powered adversaries using adaptive attack strategies. The AI essentially acts as a real-time forensic investigator, identifying both the "how" and the "why" of an attack.

Continuous improvement is the ultimate goal of incident response and forensics in a zero-trust framework. Each attack, regardless of success, provides learning opportunities. AI models are updated to incorporate new threat patterns, anomalous behaviors, and adaptive strategies observed during incidents. These updates enhance behavioral baselines, refine risk scoring, and improve predictive capabilities. Over time, the system becomes more resilient, capable of detecting increasingly subtle or novel threats that were previously undetectable.

Collaboration between AI and human analysts is essential. While AI handles speed, scale, and pattern recognition, human expertise provides contextual judgment, prioritization, and strategic guidance. Analysts review AI-generated alerts, validate containment actions, and contribute intelligence on emerging threats. This symbiosis ensures that automated defenses evolve intelligently, incorporating real-world understanding alongside computational insight.

Another critical aspect of modern incident response is integration across all digital environments. Organizations today operate across on-premises servers, cloud platforms, SaaS applications, IoT networks, and remote workforces. AI systems must correlate activity across these diverse ecosystems to provide comprehensive situational awareness. For example, a seemingly innocuous login on a cloud app may be part of a lateral movement campaign targeting sensitive databases elsewhere. By unifying telemetry, AI identifies patterns that human analysts might miss and triggers containment across affected systems.

Finally, incident response is not just about stopping attacks—it's about preparing for the next threat. Each incident refines policies, strengthens micro-segmentation, updates AI models, and informs security protocols. In a zero-trust system, learning is continuous: the network is always improving, always adapting, and always anticipating potential threats. Through a combination of AI, automated containment, forensic investigation, and human collaboration, organizations create a resilient cybersecurity posture capable of surviving and thriving in the era of AI-driven threats.

The Night of the Silent Siege

The first sign was subtle: a minor spike in unusual file access by an employee named Victor. At first glance, it seemed routine—Victor had a high-volume workload and accessed multiple servers daily. The AI, however, detected deviations in the timing and sequence of his activities. Queries were slightly faster than normal, and access patterns were inconsistent with his historical behavior. The system immediately assigned a moderate risk score and began monitoring, quietly observing every interaction.

Hours later, additional anomalies appeared. Another user account initiated unusual API calls to financial databases, and encrypted traffic was detected from a device that had never accessed sensitive data before. The AI correlated these signals across accounts, devices, and applications, identifying a coordinated attack attempt. Without alerting the attackers, the AI triggered containment measures: affected accounts were isolated, suspicious devices were quarantined, and sensitive systems were segmented from the network. Business operations continued, unaffected, while the intrusion was contained in real time.

The attackers, unaware that they had been discovered, attempted lateral movement. They probed multiple servers, escalated privileges, and tried to exfiltrate data through redundant channels. The AI detected the deviations from baseline behavior instantly, comparing it to historical patterns and global threat intelligence feeds. Risk scores increased, triggering automatic lockdowns of compromised endpoints and segmentation of affected network zones. Each move by the attackers was predicted and countered in milliseconds, making their operations increasingly inefficient.

Human analysts arrived in the security operations center as the AI continued to engage the attackers. They reviewed logs, confirmed containment actions, and traced the paths of the attempted intrusion. Using the AI's forensic data, they reconstructed the sequence of events: which accounts were compromised, which devices were infected, and which servers had been targeted. Every detail of the attack was recorded, providing a complete map for post-incident analysis and future preventive measures.

The attackers shifted tactics, deploying a more sophisticated AI-powered malware variant designed to mimic normal user activity. It attempted to blend in, randomizing queries and delaying commands to evade detection. The AI, however, had learned from prior incidents. Behavioral baselines were adaptive, risk scoring was dynamic, and predictive models anticipated the attackers' moves. Every attempt was logged, analyzed, and neutralized before it could reach critical systems.

By dawn, the attack was effectively over. The AI had contained the intrusion, captured forensic evidence, and updated its machine learning models with every detail. The human security team could now perform deeper analysis, extract intelligence for policy refinement, and strengthen defenses across the network. Victor's credentials were restored, affected devices were cleaned, and the entire system resumed normal operation without data loss or disruption.

The security team marveled at the AI's performance. It had acted faster than any human could, contained multiple attack vectors simultaneously, and learned from the encounter to prevent future incidents. The attackers had attempted a full-scale breach, yet they had left empty-handed. The network had defended itself autonomously, predicted the intruders' moves, and emerged stronger.

In the aftermath, analysts reviewed the detailed forensic reports and realized the magnitude of what had transpired. The network had not merely survived—it had adapted. Every anomaly, every deviation, and every failed intrusion contributed to continuous learning. Policies were updated, behavioral baselines were refined, and predictive defenses were enhanced. The attackers would return someday, but the system had become a living, evolving guardian, capable of detecting, containing, and neutralizing threats faster than any human or AI adversary could hope to act.

By the next week, the network had already adjusted. Minor anomalies that would have gone unnoticed before were flagged and contained automatically. Lateral movement attempts were intercepted before they could propagate. The AI had transformed the network into a resilient, self-improving ecosystem. The attackers had tried to wage a silent siege, but the AI had turned it into a rehearsal for the network's continuous improvement. The network was now smarter, faster, and stronger—an autonomous sentinel that never rested.

Chapter 10

The Future of AI-Driven Zero-Trust Security

As organizations continue to migrate to cloud platforms, adopt AI-driven workflows, and embrace increasingly connected ecosystems, the landscape of cybersecurity is evolving faster than ever. The last decade has demonstrated that perimeter defenses are insufficient, static credentials are unreliable, and traditional monitoring cannot keep pace with automated, adaptive threats. Zero-trust security, powered by artificial intelligence, represents the future: a dynamic, autonomous, and continuously learning architecture capable of defending networks against known and unknown threats. Chapter 10 examines how zero-trust is evolving, the emerging role of AI in proactive defense, and the future strategies that will define cybersecurity in an AI-dominated digital world.

The fundamental principle of zero-trust remains unchanged: never trust, always verify. But future zero-trust systems are becoming increasingly sophisticated. AI now integrates behavioral analytics, predictive modeling, threat intelligence, autonomous response, and continuous learning into a single cohesive framework. Each component enhances the other, creating a resilient system that does more than simply detect threats—it anticipates them, adapts to them, and neutralizes them in real time. The future of zero-trust lies in fully autonomous networks capable of responding to attacks faster than any human or manual system could.

Cloud-native architectures are central to this evolution. Organizations no longer operate solely on-premises; data, applications, and services reside across multiple cloud providers, SaaS platforms, and hybrid networks. AI-driven zero-trust systems continuously monitor interactions across these environments, analyzing API calls, cloud workloads, and inter-service communication. Traditional security models, built for static networks, cannot handle this scale or complexity. AI enables visibility into every layer, identifying anomalies and responding autonomously to prevent lateral movement and data compromise.

Automation is the next frontier in zero-trust. Future AI systems will not only detect and contain threats but also deploy automated remediation measures across the entire digital environment. Vulnerable endpoints can be patched dynamically, misconfigurations can be corrected automatically, and compromised accounts can be suspended or isolated without human intervention. These autonomous processes reduce the time between detection and response from hours—or minutes—to milliseconds, dramatically reducing the potential impact of breaches.

Threat intelligence will become increasingly predictive. AI systems will analyze global attack trends, dark web activity, emerging malware signatures, and geopolitical events to anticipate threats before they reach an organization. Zero-day vulnerabilities will no longer be exploited because AI can identify precursors: unusual activity patterns, small-scale probing attempts, or early signals of social engineering. The combination of predictive intelligence and behavioral analytics enables a shift from reactive defense to proactive defense.

Human collaboration remains essential, even in the AI-driven future. Security operations teams provide context, strategy, and oversight. They interpret complex threat scenarios, refine AI models, and guide policy decisions. However, AI increasingly handles routine detection, containment, and even complex decision-making processes. Humans become strategic supervisors rather than reactive responders, focusing on improving system resilience and designing policies that allow AI to operate at maximum efficiency.

Another critical trend is adaptive risk management. In the future, zero-trust systems will continuously evaluate not only actions and behaviors but also business impact, sensitivity of data, regulatory compliance, and potential financial consequences. Risk scores will guide dynamic policy enforcement. Access controls will be continuously adjusted based on evolving threats, user behavior, and operational priorities. The system becomes intelligent enough to balance security with usability, ensuring productivity is maintained while threats are contained.

Finally, the future of AI-driven zero-trust security is continuous improvement. Every incident, whether a minor anomaly or a sophisticated attack, is recorded, analyzed, and used to enhance models and policies. Networks will evolve autonomously, learning from both internal and global intelligence sources. Each attempted breach becomes a lesson; every successful containment strengthens defenses. Organizations adopting these principles will not merely survive in the era of AI-powered cybercrime—they will thrive, maintaining resilient, adaptive, and secure digital ecosystems capable of responding to threats faster than attackers can innovate.

In conclusion, AI-driven zero-trust represents the ultimate evolution of cybersecurity. It is proactive, predictive, autonomous, and continuously learning. It balances human expertise with machine precision, ensures resilience in complex, hybrid environments, and adapts to emerging threats with unmatched speed. Organizations that embrace this future will not just protect their assets—they will build networks that anticipate, respond to, and outpace the ever-evolving landscape of AI-powered cyber threats.

The Autonomous Guardian

It began on a typical Thursday morning. Across the organization's sprawling hybrid network, users logged in, applications synced, and cloud workloads executed their routines. To human observers, everything appeared normal. Yet beneath the surface, an AI zero-trust system was continuously scanning, analyzing, and learning. Every keystroke, API call, and data transfer was evaluated against dynamic baselines, threat intelligence feeds, and behavioral models. The network was alive, constantly assessing risk.

An attempted intrusion emerged within milliseconds. A malicious actor had obtained credentials from a contractor account. They tried to move laterally, first targeting a development server, then probing database access. The AI detected micro-anomalies instantly. Login patterns were slightly off, access sequences diverged from baseline behavior, and devices used did not match historical fingerprints. The system raised the risk score while isolating affected endpoints.

The attacker, unaware that they were being watched, deployed an AI-powered malware agent designed to mimic normal user activity. It attempted to blend in, randomizing queries and timing requests to evade detection. But the network's AI was faster, more precise, and adaptive. Every deviation, every small inconsistency, was logged and analyzed. Risk scores escalated, and containment measures were deployed autonomously. Sessions were restricted, affected devices quarantined, and network segments dynamically micro-segmented to prevent lateral movement.

Within seconds, the attacker attempted to pivot, targeting the financial application to extract payroll data. The AI had already predicted this move based on correlated threat intelligence from global attack trends and prior incidents. Preemptive barriers were deployed, API access was blocked, and the malware was trapped in a quarantined segment. Attempts to escalate privileges were automatically denied. The intruder became ensnared in the network's living defense system.

Human analysts arrived at the security operations center, reviewing the AI's actions in real time. They observed containment, isolation, and predictive defense in action. While the humans monitored and validated, the AI had neutralized the threat completely. No data was lost, no downtime occurred, and the attacker never reached critical systems. It was a seamless collaboration between machine speed and human oversight. Over the next few hours, the AI performed autonomous forensic analysis. Every packet, command, and file access was traced and cataloged. The system identified potential vulnerabilities, refined behavioral baselines, and updated risk models. It even detected low-level anomalies elsewhere in the network that were likely unrelated but potentially exploitable. Proactive patches were deployed, endpoints reinforced, and policy rules dynamically adjusted. The network learned from the incident, becoming more resilient.

By evening, the network was stronger than it had been that morning. Minor anomalies were already being flagged automatically, lateral movement attempts were intercepted before they could propagate, and predictive models had evolved to detect emerging threats faster. The AI had transformed the organization's cybersecurity posture, operating at a level humans could not match in speed, precision, or scale.

The attackers would likely attempt another intrusion, but the network was ready. It had become a self-improving guardian, capable of detecting, predicting, and containing threats autonomously. Every interaction, every anomaly, and every attempted breach contributed to its intelligence. The AI had proven that in the future of cybersecurity, resilience comes from systems that never sleep, never assume trust, and continuously evolve. The autonomous guardian had not merely defended the network—it had rewritten the rules of defense. It anticipated attacks, neutralized threats before they could succeed, and continuously strengthened its own capabilities. In an era dominated by AI-powered cybercrime, the network itself had become the ultimate sentry, capable of surviving and thriving against adversaries faster and smarter than any human mind alone could achieve.

Final Thoughts

Zero-Trust Security & AI Threat Monitoring

As we conclude this book, it's important to reflect on the transformative nature of zero-trust security in the modern digital age. Over the past chapters, we've explored how AI-driven systems have reshaped cybersecurity, shifting it from reactive defense to proactive, predictive, and adaptive protection. The era of static firewalls, simple password authentication, and perimeter-based trust is over. In its place, organizations must adopt a mindset that assumes nothing is safe until continuously verified. Zero-trust security combined with AI threat monitoring is no longer a luxury—it is a necessity for survival in the digital landscape.

Zero-trust architectures are built on continuous verification. Every user, device, application, and network segment is treated as potentially hostile until proven otherwise. AI acts as the nervous system of this architecture, analyzing millions of signals per second to detect subtle anomalies that humans cannot perceive. Whether monitoring behavioral patterns, predicting threat vectors, or automatically containing potential intrusions, AI ensures that risk is constantly assessed and mitigated in real time.

The combination of behavioral analytics, micro-segmentation, autonomous containment, and continuous learning forms a defense system that is resilient and self-improving. Each incident—whether it's an attempted breach, malware deployment, or AI-powered social engineering attempt—becomes a lesson. The network adapts and strengthens, making future attacks progressively more difficult. Organizations that embrace these principles do more than protect data; they create a living, adaptive ecosystem that grows stronger with every threat encountered.

We also emphasized the critical interplay between AI and human expertise. While AI excels at speed, scale, and pattern recognition, human oversight remains vital. Analysts guide policy, interpret complex scenarios, and provide strategic judgment that machines alone cannot deliver. The most effective zero-trust systems balance autonomous AI decision-making with informed human intervention, ensuring both precision and context in every response.

Proactive threat hunting is another cornerstone of modern zero-trust security. AI continuously searches for anomalies, correlates global threat intelligence with local behavioral patterns, and identifies potential attack vectors before they are exploited. The result is a system that is not merely reactive but anticipatory, capable of neutralizing threats before damage occurs. Predictive capabilities extend across endpoints, cloud services, IoT devices, AI agents, and user interactions, creating comprehensive situational awareness.

The continuous evolution of security policies and risk assessment models is what distinguishes AI-driven zero-trust from traditional approaches. Trust is no longer binary or static; it is dynamic and context-sensitive. Risk scores are continuously calculated, responses are proportionate, and access is granted or restricted based on real-time intelligence. This fluid approach ensures that the network remains secure without unnecessarily hindering legitimate operations, maintaining productivity while enforcing vigilance.

Finally, the future of cybersecurity belongs to those who adopt adaptive, AI-powered zero-trust systems. Attackers are increasingly intelligent, automated, and capable of AI-assisted strategies. Static defenses are insufficient. Organizations that implement dynamic verification, autonomous containment, predictive threat detection, and continuous learning position themselves to survive and thrive. In the era of AI-powered cyber threats, zero-trust is not a tool—it is a philosophy, a strategy, and a necessity.

This book serves as a roadmap to understanding, implementing, and leveraging AI-driven zero-trust security.

Whether you are an IT professional, cybersecurity strategist, business leader, or technology enthusiast, the principles outlined here provide the knowledge and insights needed to defend digital assets in a rapidly evolving threat landscape. Zero-trust and AI threat monitoring are the ultimate combination for modern cybersecurity—capable of defending, adapting, and evolving continuously to meet the challenges of today and the threats of tomorrow.

www.ingramcontent.com/pod-product-compliance
Ingram Content Group UK Ltd.
Pitfield, Milton Keynes, MK11 3LW, UK
UKHW020156290926
15471UKWH00005B/898